This book is written by

_____

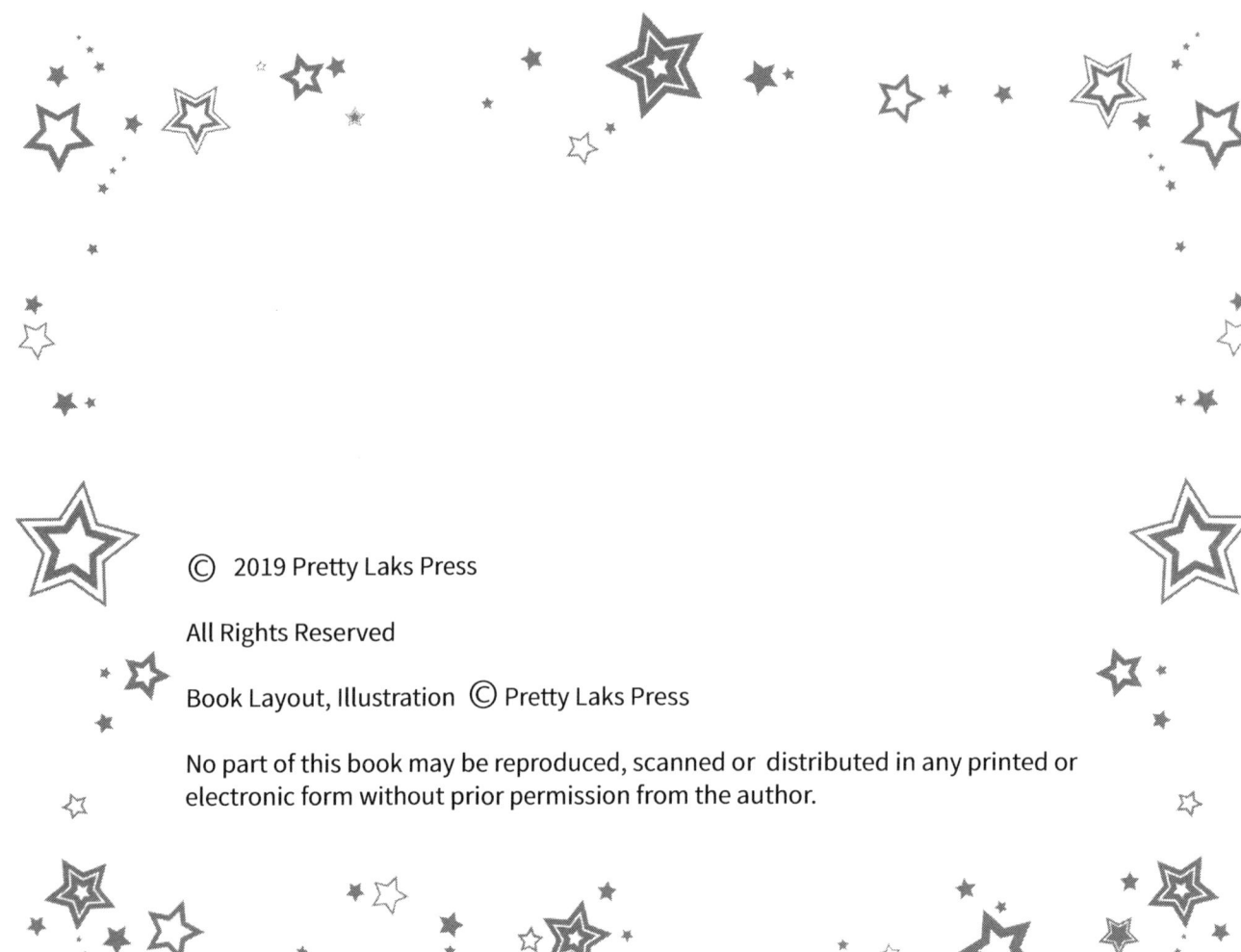

© 2019 Pretty Laks Press

All Rights Reserved

Book Layout, Illustration © Pretty Laks Press

No part of this book may be reproduced, scanned or distributed in any printed or electronic form without prior permission from the author.

You are super awesome because

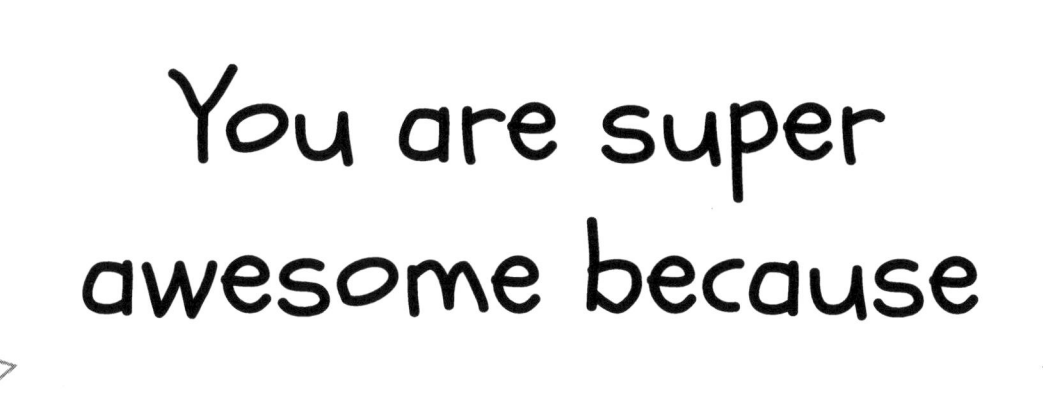

_____

I love how you

_____

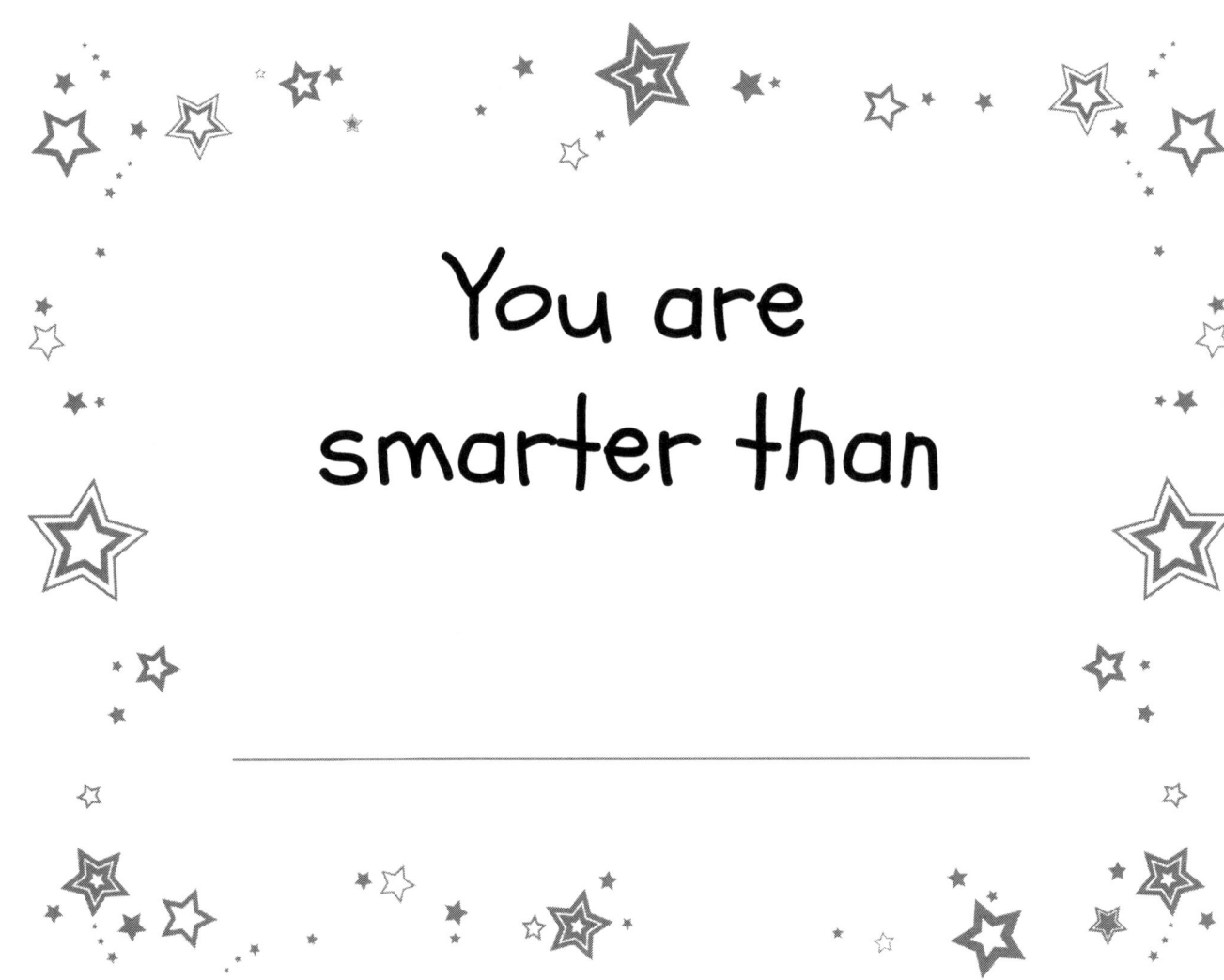

You work hard at

_____

I love when you

_____

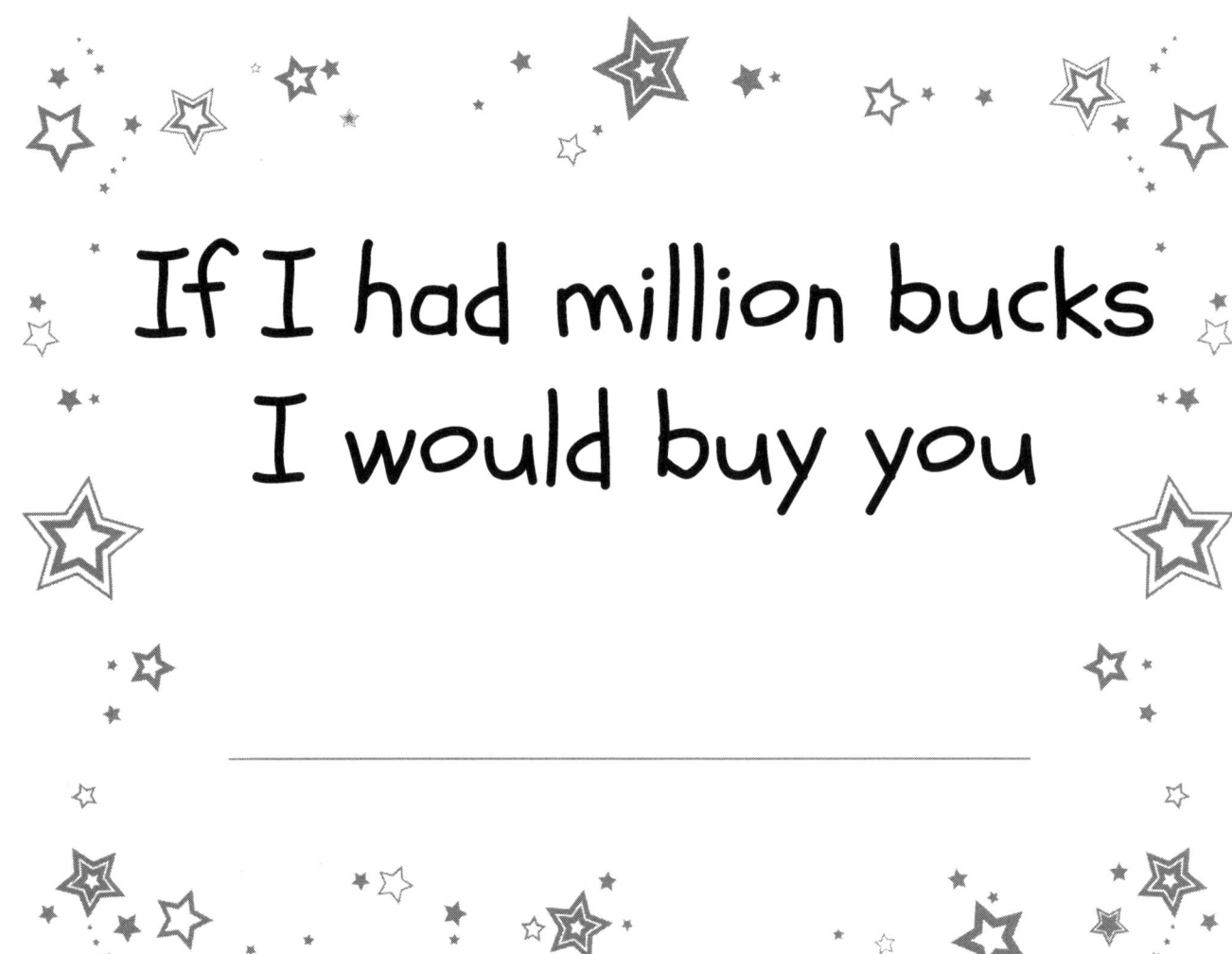

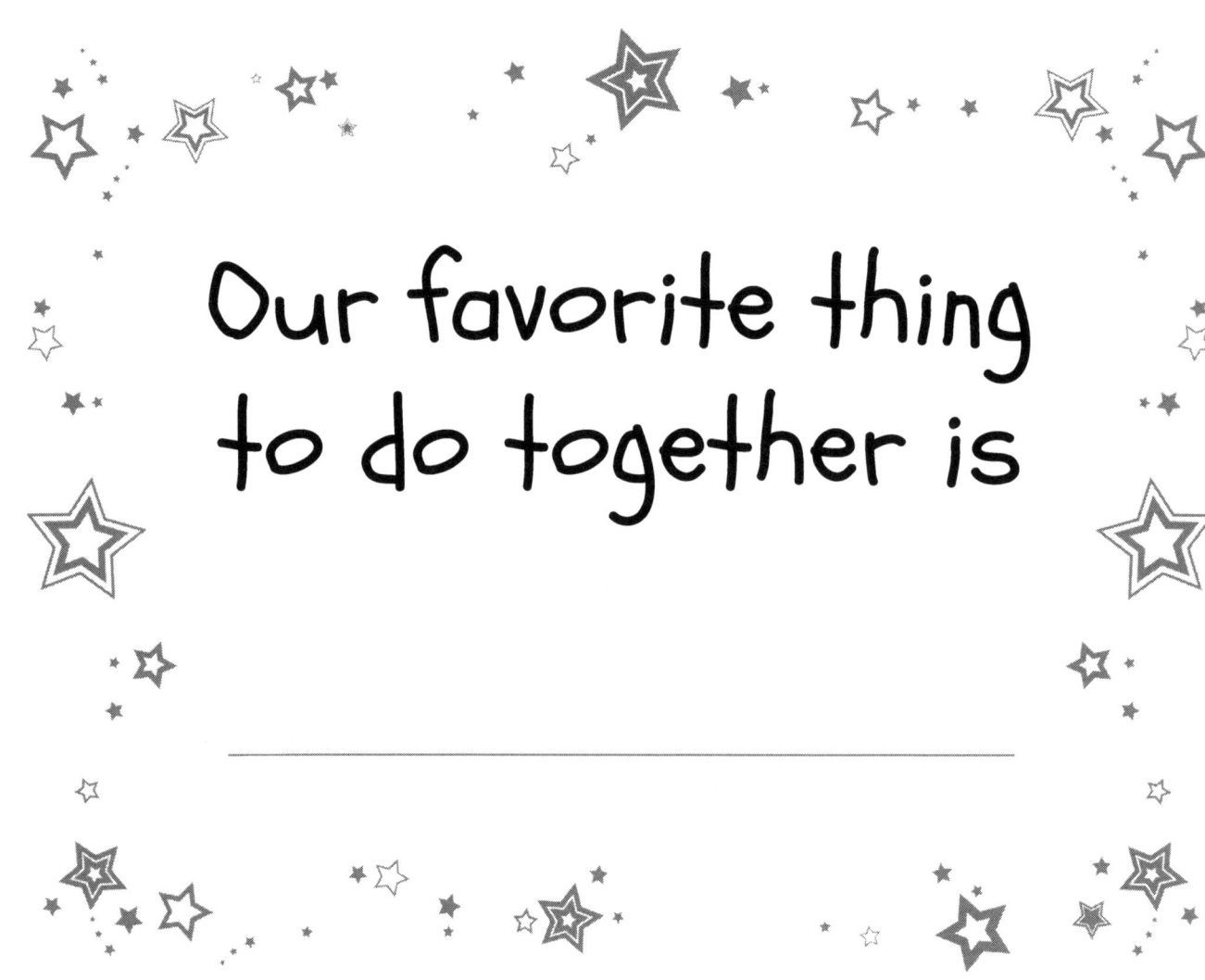

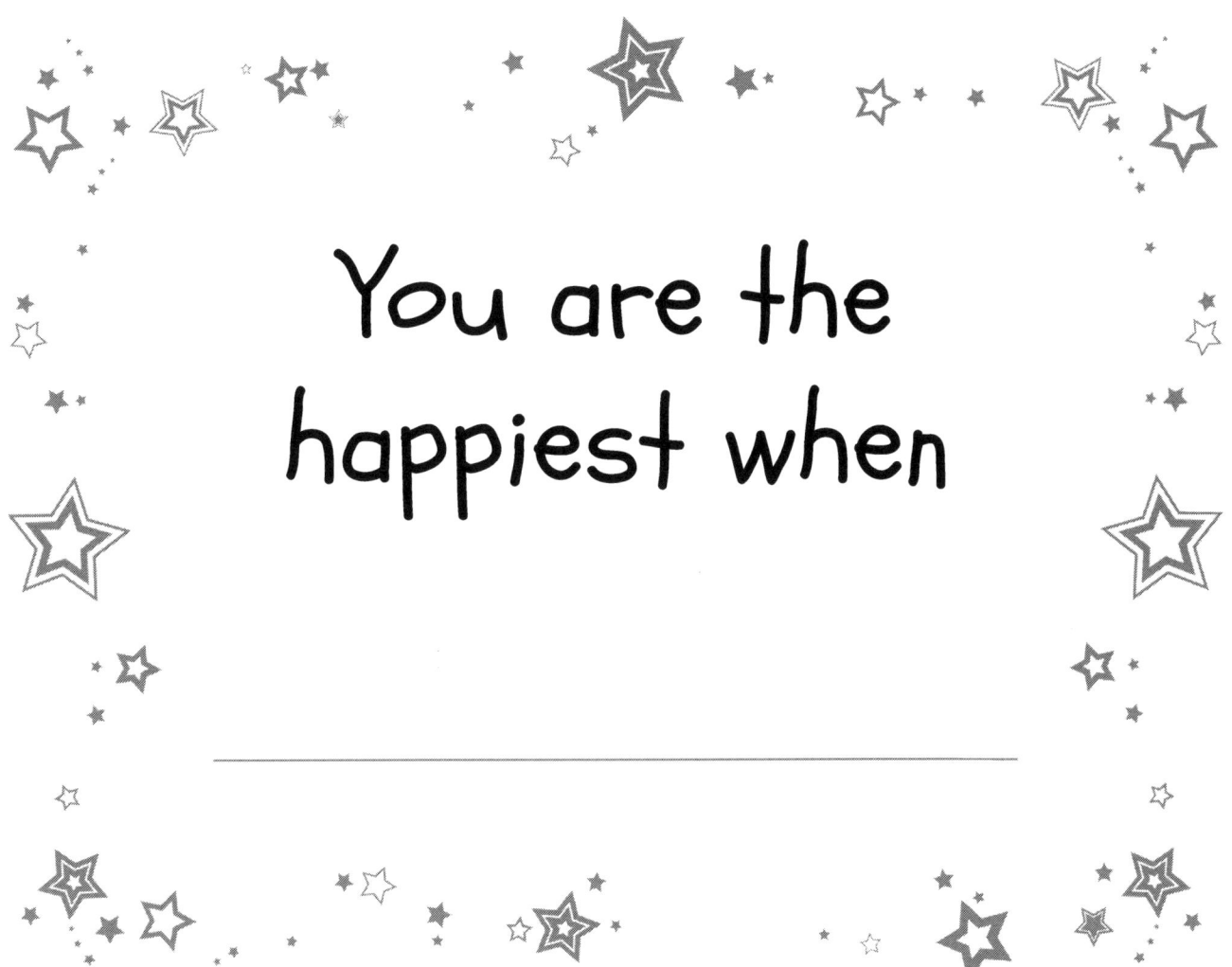

You are the happiest when

_____

I would buy you a million
_____

You love when I

_____

I wish I had your
_____

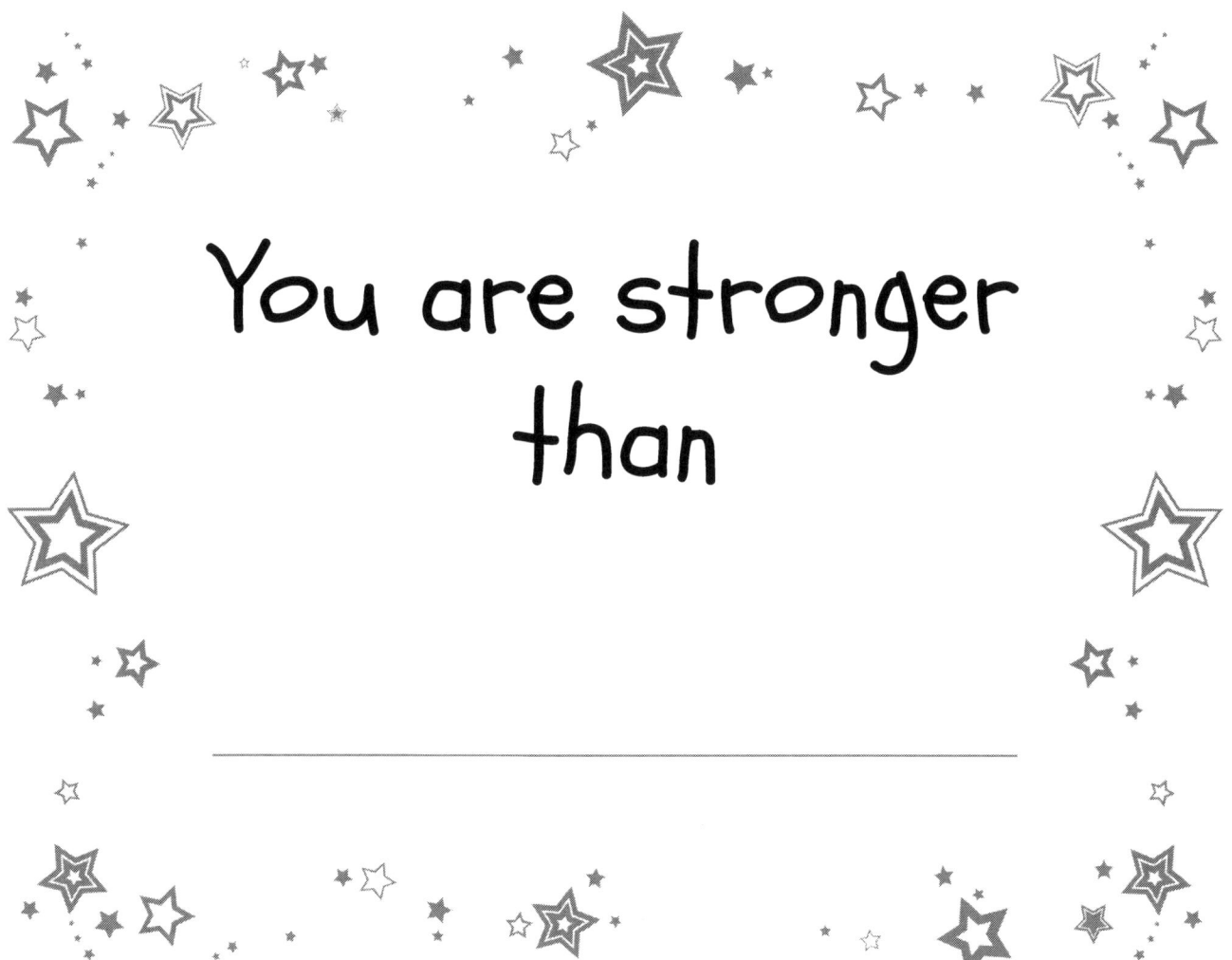

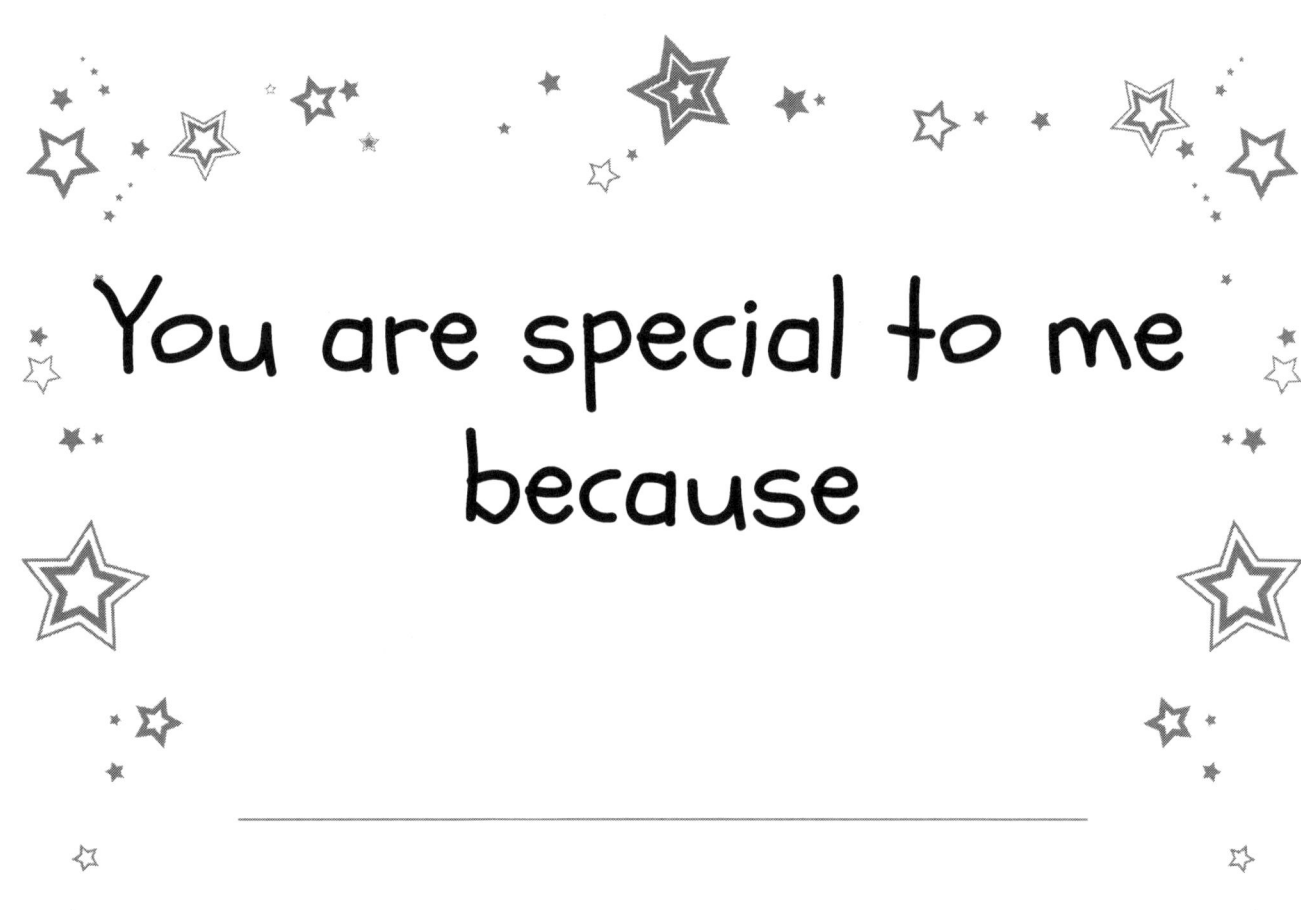

You are special to me because

_____

You make everyone

I love when you tell stories about

_____

Funniest thing you do is

_____

I wish we have more time to

_____

I was amazed when you fixed my

_____

I feel safe when you

_____

You don't care about

_____

I'm proud to say

_____

You like to read

_____

I like when you make funny

_____

I loved when you surprised me with

_____

You always say

_____

I love you more than

_____

Game I like to play with you is

_____

You are the kind of person who always

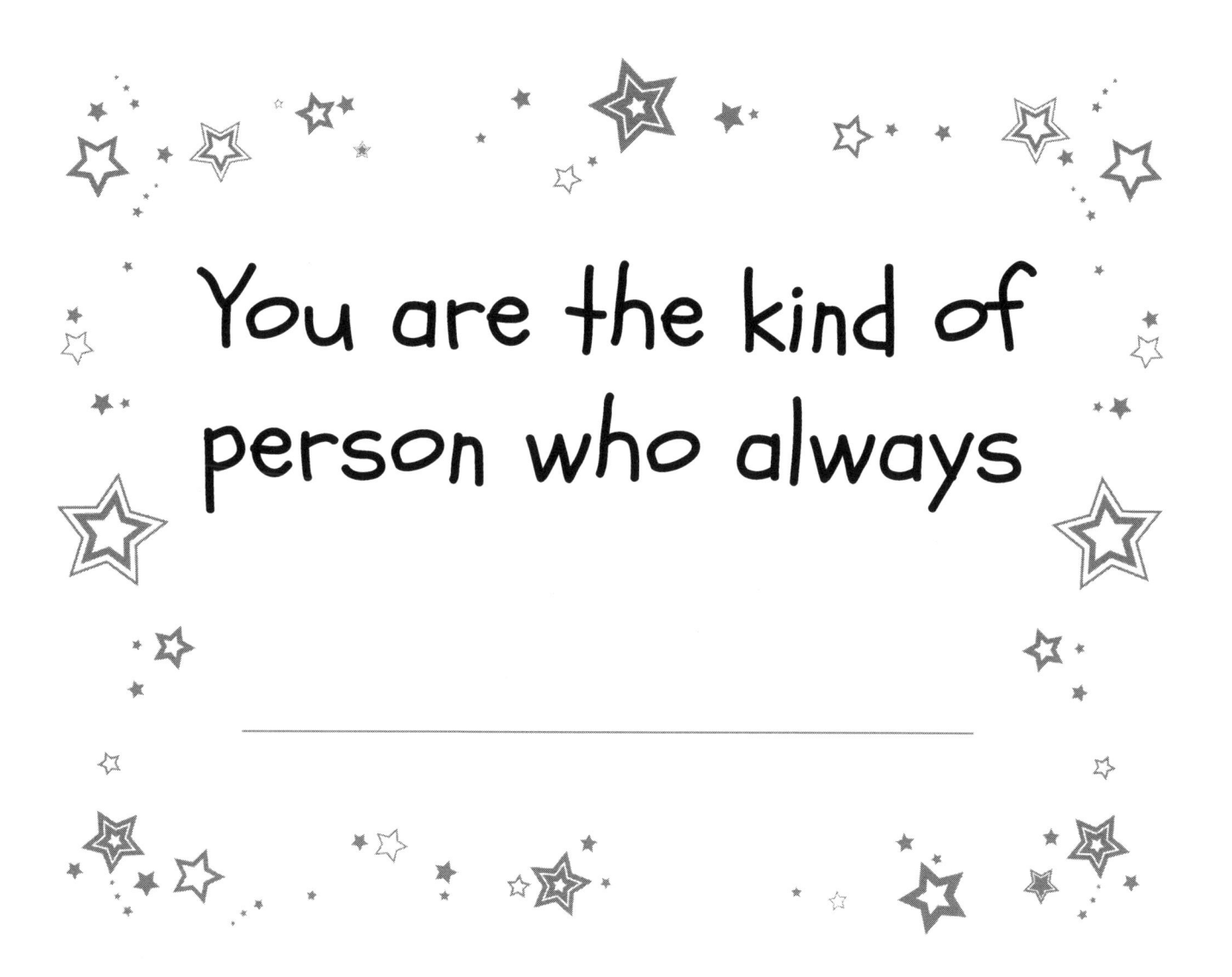

_____

You are proud of me when I

_____

You are a perfect

_____

I want you to know that I will

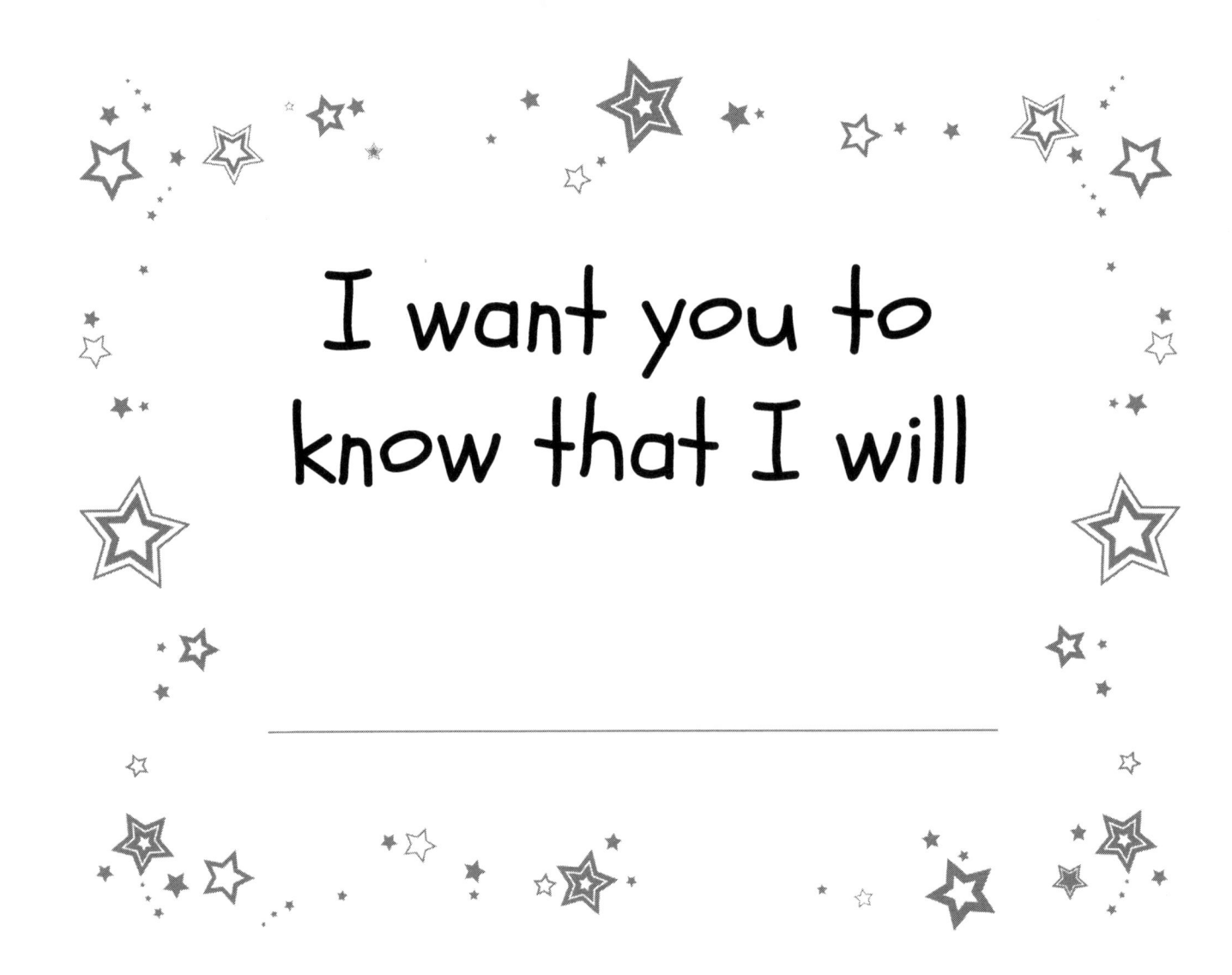

_____

Made in the USA
San Bernardino, CA
12 June 2019